A TUNNEL OF HIDDEN THOUGHTS RELEASED

A TUNNEL OF HIDDEN THOUGHTS RELEASED

Oni Shabazz

Copyright © 2022 by Oni Shabazz.

Cover design by Oni Shabazz, the author of
Eye to Eyewitness and Accounts of God's Miracle

Library of Congress Control Number: 2022908478
ISBN: Hardcover 978-1-6698-2412-1
 Softcover 978-1-6698-2411-4
 eBook 978-1-6698-2410-7

All rights reserved. No part of this book may be reproduced or transmitted in any form or by any means, electronic or mechanical, including photocopying, recording, or by any information storage and retrieval system, without permission in writing from the copyright owner.

English Standard Version (ESV)
The Holy Bible, English Standard Version. ESV® Text Edition: 2016. © 2001 by Crossway Bibles, a publishing ministry of Good News Publishers.

King James Version (Authorized Version). First published in 1611. Quoted from the KJV Classic Reference Bible, © 1983 by The Zondervan Corporation.

New International Version (NIV)
Holy Bible, New International Version®, NIV®, ©1973, 1978, 1984, 2011 by Biblica, Inc.® Used by permission. All rights reserved worldwide.

Any people depicted in stock imagery provided by Getty Images are models, and such images are being used for illustrative purposes only.
Certain stock imagery © Getty Images.

Print information available on the last page.

Rev. date: 05/06/2022

To order additional copies of this book, contact:
Xlibris
844-714-8691
www.Xlibris.com
Orders@Xlibris.com
838332

"The hidden voices in my head; flashbacks, releasing unhealthy thoughts, and they erupt like a volcano, and I am set free to verbalize."

"What consumes the mind controls your life."

Scripture

All scripture is breathed out by God and profitable for teaching, for reproof, for correction, and for training in righteousness (2 Tim. 3:16–17 ESV).

He Covered Me

Lord, you covered me through the fire
through the fire, Oh Lord, you covered me
thank you, faithful Lord, full of Mercy and Grace
you covered me like the three Hebrews boys
My God is inflammable, thank you Lord for your grace
and mercy.
You covered me!

—Oni Shabazz

CONTENTS

Dedication xi
Preface xv
A Tunnel of Hidden Thoughts Released xix

Releasing Strongholds 1
Reflecting 6
Patterns 7
Flashbacks 10
Global Reset 14
Global Reset 15
Police Brutality 18
Police Brutality (Poem) 19
We Rise 20
Image of an Old Child 21
Breathe 24
Being Born Again 29
Body, Soul, and Spirit 30
Generations 32
You and I (Poem) 34
Lineage (Family) 35
My DNA and the Trail of Tears/Family Lineage 38
The Family: "The Trail of Tears" 40
Family 42
Meet Oni Shabazz 48
My Children 50
My Faith Begins Here 52
The Whole Armor of God 55

A Spiritual Foundation	57
Transition of Faith	60
The Book (Poem)	62
Prayer	63
Beatitudes	64
Fruits of the Spirit	66
The Road to Salvation	68
Songs	70
Near (Poem)	73
Death and Awareness	75
Grief	77
Healing	79
Relocating from Las Vegas to California	82
My New Town	84
Acknowledgments	87
About the Author	89
Goodbye, Punch Bowl	91

Dedication

A Tunnel of Hidden Thoughts Released—my voice was muted, and kinesis became my forerunner. Once I called on Jesus, the gates of my mind and heart were opened, and the battle with verbal expression was released. The Lord became present and the all-powerful forerunner and gatekeeper.

This book is first and foremost dedicated to my Lord and Savior Jesus Christ and then to the community that struggled or are yet struggling with this behavioral problem of hidden communication. The Bible speaks about the power of the heart, mind, and thought. I had often put others and things ahead of God, knowingly and unknowingly. Oftentimes the response was negative even though I thought I was a good and righteous person. I consulted my Lord, and I was led in the spirit to birth this book.

I've learned the role of forgiveness and repentance toward self.

Today, I'm making a wiser decision and expressing my feelings and emotions. Believe me, I have found joy that surpasses man's traditions on how I should feel about things.

This book entails events and scenes from my past and present that appear in a narrative **out of chronological order.** I embark on sharing a chain of information, explaining something about the past or present

and people, places, and things. Much of my life reflects the way a film exposition is handled.

Roll back the curtain and let the drama begin.

Memories, of a tunnel of nonverbal communication wards intense, suppressed emotions and situations liable to burst out suddenly; painfully, scary, creepy, mind shaken, happy and sad occasions leading to internal and external damages.

Traumatic experiences that return daily in some form or another that **return to me repeatedly and link me up with the next one to come**, which is a form of **PTSD**.

This alone lets me know that without these thoughts, flashbacks, and foggy recalls, I wouldn't have a need for God. Through the Holy Spirit, all things are possible. He strengthens me, and I am never alone.

His spirit abides in me. God is a permanent resident in my body that He fashioned and molded. We must learn that Jesus walked on earth. He is a source of refuge and protection. Learning how to think, understand, and formulate thoughts is a priority. Again, life and death are of the tongue.

Establish a moral compass for your beliefs and values, aligning you with the word of God!

These are the keys to the cosmos.

Mastering your mindset can be a formidable opponent on your path to your purpose. Overcome your story. Everyone has it, and it can be life-changing. A fit brain is a smart one! I am sharing parts of my confession throughout the book. Once I opened my mouth and expressed my feeling about my past to the heavenly, I started changing from the inside out. There is hope for all who trust in the Lord. Stay encouraged.

Again, my allegiance is to God, family, extended families, friends, and you, the new addition.

I am honored to have my family and extended family in my life, as well as my new friends and readers across the globe. A special thanks to my cousin Barbara Booth for her ear to listen and the divine appointment from God Almighty.

"The Lord is My Light and Salvation—whom shall, I fear? The Lord is the strength of my life; whom shall I be afraid?" (Ps. 27:1 NIV).

"The fear of the Lord is the beginning of wisdom: a good understanding has all they that do his commandments: his praise endures forever" (Ps. 111:10 ESV).

Finally, to the loves of my life, my three most precious peas, and my grandchildren, the twins Dr. D. and Professor (the titles I gave them at an early age). They are all my reason for all seasons.

Thank You, Precious Lord!

Now I have allowed God to fix my problem by opening my mouth and asking for help.

"I can rejoice in the Lord that at last you have renewed your concern for me. Indeed, you have been concerned, but you had no opportunity to show it. I am not saying this because I am in need, for I have learned to be content whatever the circumstances. I know what it is to be in need and know what it is to have plenty. I have learned the secret of be content in any and every situation, whether well fed or hungry, living in plenty or in want. I can do everything through Him who gives me strength" (Phil. 4:10–13 NIV).

Life is an uncertain roller coaster. Challenges in life are a given, and they are used for us to grow. Each one of us has the golden opportunity for personal growth and self-improvement. Ultimately, the goal is to use everything from the Bible and the word of God to become the best version of ourselves. ***Stay encouraged!*** You can rebel against all life's trials and tribulations, resenting every moment of your journey, but **it will rob you of what God has in store for you!**

We get better with and through God. The loss helps you reflect, correct, and find opportunities to improve your jobs, relationships, family, home, and thoughts. Loss is inevitable. The key is to become a better person. It will give your words and actions integrity.

Failure helps us develop compassion, empathy, and sympathy, which are also essential for the journey.

Setbacks, mishaps, monkey wrenches, and unforeseen circumstances are forever present. Resilience is the ability to overcome setbacks, and I declare I am an overcomer. These battles don't belong to us; they belong to God. The spirit always fights with the flesh, and God is the great mediator.

Thank you, Jesus, for the knowledge and understanding. I'm no longer complaining but proclaiming all the promises of God, knowing the mind controls the heart and we overcome through prayer.

Your prayer might be, "O Lord, you hear my voice." Allow the Holy Ghost and the word to strike fire in your heart.

Preface

The cover of the book depicts a tunnel in the mind that has been held captive for decades in the subconscious.

I am inspired and hopeful today. Tomorrow I will use my momentum through this book to keep fighting spiritually for our minds, bodies, and souls. Socialization is our right. Keeping our faith in God and praying makes a difference.

We must continue to push our agenda for positive health and not lose our inability to use our voice. (Communication and self-expression are the keys to open doors.) When you don't have a voice, you must scream silently or deal with deep rage within that wreaks havoc leading us to act out. It causes depression, pills, oversleeping, overeating, drugs, alcohol, cigarettes, sin, etc.

Our fear causes us to miss the cause or overlook the root of the problem until we find ourselves in a panic room.

This is my exodus. The Lord helped and delivered me!

For the wages of sin is death, but the gift of God is eternal life in Christ Jesus, our Lord.

The optimist in you and me hope toxic people will become better. The good news is, they can. Unhealthy people can grow healthier with the proper care and attention in a healthy environment: the **word** (**Bible**).

If you don't address toxic people or, worse, let them gain a foothold or influence your mind, they can infect God's purpose, which is spreading the great commission.

A Tunnel of Hidden Thoughts Released

Definition of *nonchronological*—not of, relating to, or arranged according to the order of time.

"Nonchronological doesn't follow the normal cause-and-effect order."

I'M INVITING YOU TO SIT BACK, RELAX, AND ENJOY MY JOURNEY AS I FLACKBACK INTO *A TUNNEL OF HIDDEN THOUGHTS RELEASED*. THESE OUR THOUGHTS MY MIND HAD absorbed:

QUIET THOUGHTS, LIVING IN A FOG, SCRAPPY, PATCHWORK, REPRESSED MEMORIES.

RECALL, TRIGGERED, HIDDEN HANDS, IMAGE OF OLD CHILD, THE VOICELESS, UNEXPRESSIBLE, HOLDING THOUGHTS, EXPRESS YOURSELF, DISCONNECTED, FROM SUBCONSCIOUS TO REALITY, QUIET STORMS, TIMES, DISCOVERIES, A VOICE EMERGES, YAY OR NAY, AND A PRESENT LIFE RETURNS.

THESE ARE THE NAMES AND CHOICES I AGONIZED OVER THE PAST THREE YEARS FOR THE TITLE OF THIS BOOK.

WE SERVE AN ON-TIME GOD.

AND JUST LIKE THAT, THE NAME OF THE BOOK WAS INSPIRED BY THE HOLY SPIRIT. THE BIRTH PAIN STARTED AND "A TUNNEL OF HIDDEN THOUGHTS RELEASED."

Emerged.

THOUGHTS WITHOUT CHRONOLOGICAL ORDER.

AMEN, HALLELUJAH!

STEPPING OUT OF THE BOX AND INTO THE UNIVERSE WITH MY Lord.

A Tunnel of Hidden Thoughts Released

A Tunnel of Hidden Thoughts Released is about long-suffering because of not communicating and expressing my feelings and thoughts to others. The image of an old child is my grandson, Professor, the shadow of me, Oni, as a young teen, afraid to express or articulate feelings and thoughts. My voice, at times, was quiet but echoed in the subconscious of my mind like a tunnel running a course. This went on for decades. It made me struggle with my ability to communicate effectively.

THE QUESTION I HAD TO ASK MYSELF IS, CAN ANYBODY READ YOUR MIND?

THE ANSWER IS NO.

MY MIND SAYS, "RELEASE ME. DON'T KILL MY DREAMS."

FEAR PLAYS A MAJOR ROLE IN MY NONVERBAL COMMUNICATION.

I DIDN'T KNOW HOW TO ASK FOR HELP. I DIDN'T KNOW HOW TO EXPLAIN MY THOUGHTS. BEING PART OF THE BABY BOOMERS, WE ACTED ON FEELINGS AND EMOTIONS, NOT REALIZING THAT FOR EVERY ACTION, THERE IS AN OPPOSITE REACTION, WHICH LEADS TO CONSEQUENCE. THIS HAS IMPACTED OUR LIVES OVER GENERATIONS.

I didn't know how to make or formulate decisions, so I coped. I have learned that everything in life has protocol or order, just as God's creation.

Releasing Strongholds

"Be strong and courageous. Do not be afraid or terrified because of them, for the LORD Your God goes with you; he will never leave you or for fake you" (Deut. 31:6 ESV).

I also told my grandson that Immanuel, meaning *God with us*, has come. He's the Alpha and Omega, the beginning and the end, to wage peace and restore the earth to those called by his name!

We talk about seeking refuge in God, speaking his mind, and breaking free from this type of stronghold, and that God would lead, guide, direct, and protect our minds and hearts forever just for the asking.

This was and is the beginning of releasing hidden thoughts. For us all!

At this point in my life, I want to complain, but why bother? I have had some good days, some stormy ones, and plenty of mountains to climb, not to mention the bad ones; but with this knowledge, I can now help others overcome these situations and shortcomings. These are the things that testimonies come from.

Horrible, incredible, despicable thoughts can flourish, but we must capitulate or block them from hurting us. Facing this issue bravely and boldly takes courage that already is in us, the hope of glory.

I kissed my breath heavily, so my thoughts would not escape my lips. This pattern went on for decades. When I started observing this characteristic in people, I crossed over the years of my life. I realized this was a self-inflicted disorder. Not until I observed it in my grandson decades later that I knew I had to expose this secret so he could release the thoughts of his inner man that he had found solace in, like me, and become bold for the Lord. I explain to him that God does not give us a spirit of fear.

Second Timothy 1:7 KJV says, "For God has not given us a spirit of fear, but of power, love, and a sound mind."

We are not alone. Presently there is a community in this world dealing with these same issues and strongholds.

Praise the Lord for the revelation!

Strongholds of this type, noncommunication and non-expressions, are bad for your health. They are silent killers!

Shock, denial, anger, and blame of others must stop!

Retreating from strongholds; flashbacks, hidden thoughts are something are someone. Holding on to or concealing emotions is damaging. Giving pinnacle or release is like a diamond in the rough.

Weighty affairs of thoughts keep us going back to a set of moods; and they are resetting depression, repression, and impressions where the scheming and plotting of subliminal suggestions are ongoing and compelling.

My parents were victims, and their parents played these schemes and plots to keep their minds and thoughts quiet through brainwashing and fear. I have learned the crippling effect of fear and silence. It keeps one powerless and caged like Angelou's "caged bird," lacking success and freedom.

It's a Parable in the Gospel of Matthew 25:14–24 ESV:

> [14] For it will be like a man going on a journey, who called his servants[a] and entrusted to them his property. [15] To one he gave five talents,[b] to another two, to another one, to each according to his ability. Then he went away. [16] He who had received the five talents went at once and traded with them, and he made five talents more. [17] So also he who had the two talents made two talents more. [18] But he who had received the one talent went and dug in the ground and hid his master's money. [19] Now after a long time the master of those servants came and settled accounts with them. [20] And he who had received the five talents came forward, bringing five talents more, saying, "Master, you delivered to me five talents; here, I have made five talents more." [21] His master said to him, "Well done, good and faithful servant.[c] You have been faithful over a little; I will set you over much. Enter into the joy of your master." [22] And he also who had the two talents came forward, saying, "Master, you delivered to me two talents; here, I have made two talents more." [23] His master said to him, "Well done, good and faithful servant. You have been faithful over a little; I will set you over much. Enter into the joy of your master." [24] He also who had received the one talent came forward, saying, "Master, I knew you to be a hard man, reaping where you did not sow, and gathering where you scattered no seed, [25] so I was afraid, and I went and hid your talent in the ground. Here, you have what is yours." [26] But his master answered him, "You wicked and slothful servant! You knew that I reap where I have not sown and gather where I scattered no seed? [27] Then you ought to have invested my money with the bankers, and at my coming I should have received what was my own with interest. [28] So take the talent from him and give it

> to him who has the ten talents. ²⁹ For to everyone who has will more be given, and he will have an abundance. But from the one who has not, even what he has will be taken away. ³⁰ And cast the worthless servant into the outer darkness. In that place there will be weeping and gnashing of teeth."

Yet we must fight for every sunrise and sunset, every tic of our spiritual or eternal clock. The Bible says there is a time for all seasons. Pathfinders look to the elements to find paths.

If the path withholds breathtaking or unsurmountable beauty, let us not concentrate on where the path ends. Stay focused and allow yourself to see with compassion and clarity the blooming of the flowers and a potpourri of dried petals placed in bowls or small sacks to perfume clothing or a room.

If we view the mountains, they're always surrounded by helpmeets of winding paths. The journey is our reward. But if we start to harbor the wisdom or direction of the journey, it could escape us and set us back into darkness. Considering life and death are of the tongue. Therefore, clarity of mind keeps our thought; communication free and feeling healthy. We are learning to let go those elements that keep us in the mud of civilization, especially the fearful ones.

Secrets kept for a prolonged period can result in ill will and become deadly or harmful, and we miss the mark. The cemetery is the most fertile because some of the greatest gifts on earth were never communicated because of fear. They just did not know how to express them! Open the door of your mind and heart, casting all cares on Abba Father!

God loves us and all His creations.

Victory is ours for the asking, no matter how we feel. Thank You, Lord, for walking and carrying us when we don't know it. Sometimes we find ourselves in unexpected places visiting unexpected people to share promises made by our Heavenly Father, the God of Abraham, Isaac, and Jacob.

He allows our helping hands to be a blessing to others. Like gravity, what goes up must come down. Like an overload of forgiveness, we must forgive seven times seventy or 490 times a day!

May we always trust in God's faithfulness. He will never let us down, and he's always on time. May He bring conviction to His people and bestow trust and hope for a dying world. God is my friend, my lover, and my life. He is my oasis, my sunshine for every tomorrow, and my father among perennial parents. When I cry, He dries my teary eyes, and He teaches me how to love myself. Most importantly, He listens to my innermost thoughts. He can do the same for you!

Reflecting

I thank God who always has a ram in the bush for you. On September 14, 2010, I received a call from Mary. I spoke, and she immediately told me to call 911. I told her, "I'm okay, just can't get warm." I was freezing, covered with several blankets wrapped around me and the heater blasting to its maximum. I told her, "I will take a hot bath or shower." She screamed, telling me not to get in the water. She insisted that I call 911, so I agreed to get her off the phone. I thought that she's getting on my nerves.

I was told Mary called our friend John and told him that I was severely ill and that she heard it in my voice while we were talking on the phone. He didn't believe it because he had seen me hours earlier, and I had appeared to be okay, but he called 911, and they met up at my place in Vegas.

It turned out I ended up in the hospital and slipped into a coma because of a kidney stone. Yes, they said I flatlined twice. My family was called to say goodbye and pull the plug.

I had the Great Works Ministries family. God blessed me with a host of witnesses and family. In 2012, my first book was published. Before, I was sent to Sacramento to rehabilitate. This period of my life reminded me of the physical, mental, and spiritual hurt and pain because I didn't express my struggles. Now I can reflect with joy on what God brought me through.

Patterns

I was told that as we think, we change the physical nature of our brain. As we purposely direct our thinking, we flush out toxic **patterns** of thinking to replace them with healthy thoughts.

"Do not copy the behavior and customs of this world, but let God transform you into a new person by changing the way, you think. Then you will learn to know God's will for you, which is good and pleasing and perfect" (Rom. 12:2 KJV).

"Change your mind" is the central theme of Jesus's first sermon (Matt. 4:17 KJV).

"Life doesn't always fit into a neat, orderly pattern."

A pattern is a regularity in the world. It's made by God's creation and repeated by human-made designs or abstract ideas. Patterns repeat in a predictable occurrence and can be observed.

Patterns come in all kinds of ascending and descending orders; they rule numbers and alphabets. They come in sequences. These are concept rule. They come in sizes, signs, and symbols. There are many kinds of patterns in the world, seen or unseen.

My concentration is on behavioral patterns, whether they are learned by brainwashing, guidance, mimicking, or peer pressure. These are helpful or harmful. They play a role in blessings and curses.

In my life, I see both blessings and curses. It started with my paternal parents, and I fostered some of these habits and behavioral issues. Unknown to me, they were passed on to my children and grandchildren. Thank you, Holy Spirit, for now, I see! Regrettably, I ask my children to forgive me for my lack of child-rearing skills, ability to communicate effectively, and attitude on how we should live. We're always cloning other ideas because society said it looks good and it was normal.

My selection of a mate or a significant other felt in the same ballpark. I was attracted to men who reminded me of my father, and the relationship appealed to me. But for them, it was more about their lives than their family lifestyle. Like my father, I wanted to be a part of the haves even though they made me struggle and juggle. The old saying "robbing Peter to pay Paul" became stable in my life because I had to have a new car every year even if the interest was just as high as the actual note on the car. Like mother, I was strict and stern, so my children and I didn't develop unbreakable bonds because of the lack of knowledge on my part. Going forward, I'm sharing all that I learned, new or old, through the word of God.

With this, the chains of patterns had to be broken, and God's word broke every chain of patterns that disconnected us, and our relationships have been restored.

New hope resides within us. Thank you, Lord Jesus, for breaking every chain and pattern that doesn't reflect your walk.

My granddaughter just texted me today, Sunday, November 7, 2021. The text reads,

Happy Sabbath day (aka) Happy Sunday as today is filled with God's blessings all over I'm sending you love, and thank you Nana for being the best grandma, teacher, and best friend, I can possibly have, as this date represent God's completion and the seventh day God used to complete His creation, bring earth and humanity together as a whole.

DR. D, age 20

I pray your family is restored through this testimony! My thoughts are the word and joy of the Lord that is inexpressible.

This Too Shall Pass

A simple phrase came from the ring designed for King Solomon. It was an inscription in Hebrew that said "Gam ze ya'avor," which means "This too shall pass away." It can bring comfort and sometimes resolution to all.

I know my family is on the road to salvation!

Flashbacks

Gee, the time has allowed me to flash back to insurmountable things, especially my significant relationships and marriages. My body trembled when the clouds of revelation confronted me on how I handled them, and I wasn't pleased with my behavior.

As I share and peel back layers of emotional madness, somewhere in my life, I didn't have the patience to deal with or forgive others for their shortcomings. Although I took the marriage vow, I can recall one marriage lasting less than a year. It was Halloween night. My husband and I were having dinner when we heard a knock on the door. I thought it's the kids, so I grabbed some candy from the bowl for the trick-or-treaters. What happened next was a wow moment.

The trick was on me. A young woman stood at my door, demanding to talk to my husband. I invited her into our home and asked her if she would like to join us for dinner. She replied, "No, thank you!" I felt something right away. Here I was in the seventh month of my pregnancy.

She wanted to talk to him in private. He asked if this would be okay. I agreed. Twenty minutes later, he returned and informed me that the woman was three months pregnant by him. At the time, I didn't know her name. I was speechless; truthfully, I just didn't know how to express myself. I had just turned twenty years early this month. We were both quiet. You could hear a pin drop. The silence was so deafening, and despair set in within me.

The next morning, he left for work, and I dressed. I took the wedding rings off and left them on the kitchen table. I knew that it was over as far as I was concerned. My thoughts were if he cheated on me once at this early stage in the marriage, he would do it again. I left and went to mother's house in Stockton from Sacramento and stayed there for two weeks to figure out my next move. I did pray, but I didn't give in to God completely. I was on that level at the time.

I didn't share my situation with mother. As far as she was concerned, I was visiting. I knew she knew something was wrong, but she never asked, and I lacked the communication skills to tell her. The marriage was annulled, I found out later. Yes, I had a baby boy that year in December 1972. I found out that the husband I thought I was in love with married her, and two years later, they were divorced.

I ran across her years later at the YMCA, where both of our children were learning to swim. She approached me and asked for my forgiveness, and I told her I forgave her a long time ago. She also told me that she was a Christian and followed Jesus's walk for her life's purpose.

I reflect on my inability to cook or drive. I decided that driving was a must, so I went to driving school and obtained my driver's license. Believe me, I was yet praying for guidance and help on all the things that would make life worth living.

Three years later, I married again to the late Professor E. He was spiritual and intelligent. He majored in English at Chico State University. He was also a poet. Little did he know he kept me in the dictionary to decipher the meaning of the words he would use. I assumed the world of humility to keep me from voicing my opinion. Even if I did have an inaudible one, I kept it pretty much to myself.

In 1979, Earl was murdered. During the funeral service, when it was time to lower the coffin, the door swung open; and his body slipped out onto the dirt. I stood frozen, yet I could see the looks on the people's faces. The crowd had been ushered to another side.

And this is how I was introduced to grieving. Grief adsorbed me for several years. I had help from people I didn't know, and I promised the Lord I would help others, and that's what I've been doing. If someone had told me this would be part of my purpose decades ago, I would have said nope, not this, no way.

I know it's part of my assignment from the Lord that I am very passionate about serving others.

Reflecting and moving forward, I was married back in 2005. It had its ups and downs. The army played a major role. **Posttraumatic stress disorder** (**PSTD**) is a psychiatric disorder that may occur in people who have witnessed a traumatic event such as war and combat. I wasn't aware of the aftermath of this mental disorder and the scars that it left behind.

While we were sleeping one night, I had a blow to my head out of nowhere. I turned over and hit him back. I realized he was dreaming he was in combat. He wanted to know why I hit him. I told him what had happened. He apologized, and I did too. Since that night, I have watched his behavior and its triggers. His anxiety levels were out of control. The backfiring of a car would trigger him back to combat. Yet he enjoyed war movies.

Therefore, I live with his combat too. He died in January 2015 from a heart attack. As I reflect, I see the lesson in my behavior as well. In God's kingdom, we all have a role to perform in the family. The ingredients missing on my part were the fruits of the spirit.

I was too busy saying, "You don't tell me what to do," "Where did the respect go?" or "How did it get there?"

Forgive me, Father. The old saying goes, "When you know better, you do better."

Lesson well learned.

Global Reset

The Lord is righteous in all his ways and loving toward us all he made.

The Lord is near to all that calls on him, all that calls him in truth.

He fulfills the desires of those who fear him; he hears their cry and saves them.

The Lord watches over all who love him, but all the wicked he will destroy.

My mouth will speak in praise of the Lord. Let every creature praise his name forever and ever. (Ps. 145:17–21 KJV)

We can reset our minds because God is global!

Global Reset

Example of lack of communication. Regaining freedom from this COVID-19 virus and experiencing influx of illness and death. If communicated in a timely matter, would or could it have changed anything?

THE COVID-19 PANDEMIC IMPACTED THE WORLD. THE OUTBREAK REARED ITS UGLY HEAD SOMETIME IN THE LATTER PART OF 2019.

The new vaccine rolled out in December 2020, approximately one year after the devastation of COVID-19. Being laid-back, secluded, and quarantined made us feel uncertain about the vaccines rolling out: Pfizer, Moderna, Johnson & Johnson. Gut instincts make us think, is this really happening, or is this part of a mirage, and are we safe from man and lab?

Have you forgotten the Red Sea?

Things that trigger or negate feelings of danger or solitary confinement keep us wondering what frailty awaits us. Are we looking at a one-world order?

It ensues encampment or forced social distancing, shelter in place, and quarantine. NOW, home feels like a prison. Are we in the devil's punch bowl? This virus has no respect for people, gender, age, creed, or color. No one is exempt!

I have family members stricken with COVID-19 on February 2, 2021, and are still having side effects, such as not being able to smell. On September 19, it struck another family member, and his experience was tumultuous. It reduced him down to like an infant who couldn't hold a cup. The pain was so severe. There are other people's testimonies.

To the global families, my heartfelt condolences during this time of bereavement as we know that the Comforter is always a present help to comfort and strengthen us. Holy Spirit, guide our thoughts and help us to celebrate a spirit at rest.

May we walk by faith and finish our purpose in the land of the living.

We are not looking at a period of calm. We are a long way away.

Globally, we are a long way from winning the fight against viruses if man is in the labs. The rich only becomes richer, and depopulation becomes the order of the era.

We have had various epidemics, plagues, and other contagious diseases in ages past, and some still exist. Several viruses have jumped from animal to human and contributed to the loss of countless lives, which called for antiviral drugs, safe or not. They have also bred a wave of anxiety and panic and lost communication among families globally.

Because of the nature of the virus and its variants (Delta and Omicron), we must move spiritually to a new or uncharted or unknown platform and let go and let God and trust the Holy Spirit to lead and guide us.

META OR MEGA VERSE IS FORTHCOMING THROUGH MAN'S HANDS!

The *metaverse* (a portmanteau of *meta* and *universe*) is a hypothesized iteration of the internet, supporting persistent online 3D virtual environments through conventional personal computing, as well as virtual- and augmented-reality headsets.

The Robotic Age is fast approaching. Job security is at risk!

The Robotic Age is here in full throttle!

All these things have climaxed us into thinking and asking the Lord, **what should we do?**

Time is like a swift transition technically, and plagues have always been around. God has always been around too!

The Bible says, "If my people, which are called by my name, shall humble themselves, and pray, and seek my face, and turn from their wick ways; then will I hear from heaven, and will forgive their sin, and will heal the land" (John 3:16 NIV).

I pause to listen to Tasha Cobbs Leonard sing "You Know My Name." Lord, I'm saying it still amazes me that I'm your child. Amen!

I too love the diversity in the body of Christ and the anointing that truly rests on it. Praise the Lord.

And a good hallelujah!

Police Brutality

In the Bible, all forms of violence are considered an offense against God and humanity. The scripture is full of condemnations of violence. Time and again, violence is associated with wickedness and condemned as "detestable to the Lord" (Ps. 11, Prov. 3, 10).

All lives matter! Black lives matter, yet blacks are killing blacks as well. Where is the power in this scenario?

The attention given by President Joe Biden and former president Barack Obama affected the masses.

The result proclaims the day of justice for all again. The momentum brought by the death of George Floyd sets history for generations to come. It's a legacy through another's pain and death.

The small pivots labored in love widen the scope for **hope**!

Police Brutality

My name is Man
I have the Fans
Looking for the man (Jesus)
With the power in his hands

I am not a Nigger
I'm so much Bigger
So, keep your hand off the Trigger

I CAN'T BREATHE!!!
Dedicated to all the Floyds of the world.

We Rise

[8] If your hand or your foot causes you to stumble, cut it off and throw it away. It is better for you to enter life maimed or crippled than to have two hands or two feet and be thrown into eternal fire (Matt. 18:8 NIV).

I saw a note on Facebook, which started with these lines: "Nothing should go back to normal."

Normal wasn't working in the past, and if we go back to the way things were, we will have lost the lesson.

We rise and do better. Yes, we rise! I can hear Angelou saying, "We rise."

As we shift the narrative, let us let go and let God!

Image of an Old Child

MY GRANDSON WAS THE KEY TO UNLOCKING THE DOORS AND REMOVING THE HEAVINESS OF CHAINS HIDDEN AND COVERED FOR MOST OF MY LIFE.

NOW I HAVE BEEN SET FREE TO HEAR MY THOUGHTS OUT LOUD, MEMORIES THAT I INTENDED TO TAKE TO MY GRAVE LIKE SO MANY OTHERS HAVE DONE ALREADY.

IF I CAN HELP ONE PERSON BREAK FREE FROM THIS TYPE OF SELF-ADDICTION OR BONDAGE, TO GOD BE THE GLORY! *SHARING IS A BLESSING AND MY PURPOSE!*

I EXPERIENCED DECADES OF ISSUES WITH COMMUNICATING AND EXPRESSING MY VIEWS, AND I SAW THEM THROUGH MY GRANDSON OF EIGHTEEN. THE UNIVERSE PAUSED, AND MY MIND AND EYES CAME ALIVE IN THAT INSTANT. THE GUILT AND SHAME I FELT WERE SURREAL. ALTHOUGH I WAS ABLE TO EXPRESS MYSELF ENOUGH TO GET BY, IT STILL HINDERED MY GROWTH FOR COMPLETE SUCCESS. THIS BLEW ME BACK TO REALITY! THE SAYING "WE DIE FROM LACK OF KNOWLEDGE" CAME BACK TO ME.

"IMAGE OLD CHILD" IS A TITLE COINED BY (FAMILY MEMBER) THE LATE CHARLES ZITT JOHNSON.

I DISCUSSED WITH CHARLES ALL I SAW AND HEARD FROM MY GRANDSON AND MY DAUGHTER.

SHE WAS DOING ALL THE TALKING. HE WAS RESPONDING, YET IT WAS INAUDIBLE. THIS WAS A VERSION OF ME REINCARNATED IN A TWINKLING OF THE EYE.

LONG STORY SHORT, MY DAUGHTER AND HER SON WERE HAVING A ROUND-TABLE DISCUSSION ABOUT LIFE. I WAS THE THIRD PARTY WITHOUT PREJUDICE. A ONE-WAY DIALOGUE FOLLOWED, AND IT WENT ON AND ON FOR WELL OVER AN HOUR. HER SON WAS ANSWERING HER QUESTIONS, BUT THEY WEREN'T AUDIBLE. THAT WAS ME, ONI, AND MOTHER WHEN I WAS AROUND SEVENTEEN. AN "IMAGE OLD CHILD" WAS *born!*

KEEP IN MIND THAT HEARING THOUGHTS IMPRISONED IN THE MIND IS NOT ALWAYS A SIGN OF MENTAL ILLNESS BUT A BEHAVIORAL ISSUE. THERE IS A COMMUNITY OF US WITH THE SAME MINDSET—INVISIBLE, IMPRISONED THOUGHTS HIDDEN IN THE DEEP TREADS OF OUR MINDS, READY TO ERUPT.

SOME TOOK THESE PRECIOUS GIFTS OF COMMUNICATION TO THEIR GRAVES. OTHERS SETTLED FOR LIVING IN THE BOX. YET OTHERS ARE CRYING OUT FOR HELP!

THE GOOD NEWS IS HELP IS HERE, AND IT HAS ALWAYS BEEN HERE THROUGH THE BIBLE AND THE WORD OF GOD. I JUST NEEDED TO ASK!

CHARLES, BEING AN AUTHOR, WROTE A POEM CALLED "BREATHE" IN MY BOOK, *EYE TO EYEWITNESSES AND ACCOUNTS OF GOD'S MIRACLE.*

I AM SHARING "BREATHE" AGAIN BECAUSE THE MESSAGE IS RELEVANT TO THE WORLD.

Breathe

Take air into the lungs and then expel it, especially as a regular physiological process. "Breathe in through your nose."

(Of a fish) draw in water with dissolved oxygen through the mouth and force it out through the gills.

"You will see the gills over opening and the gills fluttering, as water is drawn over the gills and the fish breathes."

(Of a cell, tissue, or living organism) exchange gases, especially by means of diffusion process.

"Adult amphibians also breathe through their skin."

Just as God breathed into man's nostrils! (Gen. 2:7 NIV)

"Then the Lord God formed man of the dust of the ground and breathed into his nostrils the breath of life; and man became a living soul" (Gen. 2:7 NIV).

B
Breathe in oxygen into your bloodstream, your heart, and your brain. (This is a physiological need.) Breathing allows another second and a little more time for the body to heal and adjust to what is going on inside

while pumping blood from the heart into the brain. Your blood needs oxygen, and so does your brain. (Consult a physician to verify this fact.)

Spiritually, you are breathing in life, and another second to receive the comfort of the Holy Spirit in remembrance of the word of God. Breathe in all good things and allow yourself to be comforted. (Each second counts.)

R

Release, relax, restore, relieve, and revitalize. When you exhale for a second or two, you release the pain, hurt, sadness, worry, and turmoil of your present situation; you can relax, and your heartbeat is restored to a calmer level. Exhaling gives momentary seconds of relief and aids your body in the revitalization process. Remember, a single breath lasts for only a second or two; you should continue to breathe. When you exhale, you are releasing all at the feet of Jesus so that he can bear your burdens.

E

Energy—breathing lets you take in more energy to refocus, get up, and become active or, if needed, call for help.

Empathy—why empathy? With a second of breath, try to focus and have empathy for what God is doing/has done for you or your loved one(s) now. We see in a mirror dimly, but face-to-face, we shall see clearly what God has in store for us (Paul).

Evaluation—a deep slow breath can supply a precious second to step back and get a clear look at our circumstances. You can use that breath to call upon your faith in God to help you through to the next moment and the next and so on. Through the Holy Spirit, we can lean on the hope of eternal life and understand that even if we are absent from the body, we are present with the Lord.

A

Apply your faith, belief, knowledge, and the ability to "let go and let God." This must be applied with every breath you inhale and exhale. Apply this self-comforting method to your ability to comfort others. Find the strength in Christ to be his partner in the healing process. Be comforted by him in faith, "for without faith it is impossible to please God."

T

Talk to someone who can help. Many may mean well, but not everyone can help. Find someone you trust and, basically, who has a sound mind. The best comforter is a good listener. The Lord will put someone in your life who can help you cope. Be available!

Take another breath; please remember to breathe. Take your time to cry or mourn. It's okay to cry; just allow yourself to cry a little at a time and not grieve uncontrollably. Occupy your mind with other things. (This is not a new concept, but it works.)

Laugh and smile. Don't think you are disrespecting the memory of your loved one by having a good laugh. Laughter is a short relief from the tears, and it will help you to focus on how to best honor that person. So go ahead and watch funny movies, sit with friends and family, tell humorous stories in good taste, or just watch a funny cartoon. Whatever makes you smile can also help to relax you. *Breathe!*

H

Hold on! Each breath is another second to keep on living. Breathe in slowly and then release smoothly and flowingly. Repeat the process every time you feel the hurt and/or pain building up. Remember to give yourself one extra time to heal and be comforted. Use your method of breathing to assist others who are grieving. Become a hospice assistant; again, occupy your time. Helping others can be therapeutic. We are disciples of Christ. If we do not have the spirit of God in us, we are none of his.

Hope—have hope in eternal life. Jesus said, "I am the life and the resurrection; though ye be dead ye shall live." Encourage one another. Know that you don't have to say goodbye; just say, "Until I see you again!"

E

Finally, *enable*. When you breathe in the fresh and new, you discard the old and corrupt. Breathe in new love, new hope, new joy, new air, new spirit, new faith, and new life; then exhale hurt, sorrow, tears, pain, anger, hopelessness, doubt, shame, unforgiveness, confusion, conflict, and all negative things. When you exhale hurt, you enable the birth of anger. If anger is enabled, it cannot instill unforgiveness. Unforgiveness brews up hatred. Hatred is destructive and brings death. In short, breathing can dispel and make evil null and void. Let your mind be renewed in Christ Jesus so that your sorrows can be turned into joy.

Thank You.

All scripture is breathed out by God and profitable for teaching, for reproof, for correction, and for training in righteousness (2 Tim. 3:16–17 ESV).

"When his breath departs, he returns to the earth; on that very day his plan perish" (Ps. 146:4 ESV).

This is how amazing God's creation is!

"Breathe" and "Image Old Child" were predestined and foreordained!

Breath and thoughts both apply to life. We need the wisdom of these words today. People are dying today more than ever. Sickness has reached ciphers alone with the presents grieving. We are capsulated around the world because of COVID-19 and its variants at an alarming rate.

I hope this message inspires those who need it. Tenaciousness is our ledger with divine intervention, overcoming obstacles in this mask-wearing world. "Alerts and news breaks" are seen around the world at a consistently high warning level.

Speaking of a new heaven, are we prepared? The Bible says we perish from lack of knowledge. The metaphor we constantly die spiritually and mentally takes on a physical trait.

We need to feed on love, that old traditional Christmas cup that feeds the masses nutrients and compassion once a year. Don't forget Thanksgiving, which is second in line it to give hand to tradition of plenty food for all even the homeless. These should be everyday events.

Yet our God feeds and takes care of our needs unconditionally, and it's given freely for the asking and always has—no special event needed!

Matthew 17:20 ESV speaks on the faith of a mustard seed that can move mountains.

"Have I not commanded you? To be strong and courageous. Do not be frightened, and do not be dismayed, for the Lord your God is with you wherever you go!" (Josh. 1:9 ESV).

"LORD, TEACH US THE THINGS WE WOULDN'T SEE WITH THE NATURAL EYE BUT BY THE SPIRIT OF GOD!"

In my mind and now audibly, I'm singing Gladys Knight's rendition of "Lord, you're the best thing that ever happened to me" with a smile.

Being Born Again

Being born again means having three beings: you are a spirit, you have a soul (mind) and will (emotions), and you live in a body. Jesus refers to this in a conversation with Nicodemus (John 3:3–7 ESV).

Jesus said to him, "You must reborn again. What is born of flesh is flesh, and what is born of the spirit is spirit."

This is a spiritual rebirth process. In becoming a new creature or new creation, old things pass away, and all things become new as far as God is concerned.

I never want my children to be saddled down with my baggage but to let go and let God and massacre that junk with all the positive things of God step by step. Now I know that God orders our steps.

I always possessed a natural tendency for sharing and caring. That is the godly side of me that I wanted my children to inherit. Being born again gives me this opportunity to share with the next generation.

Body, Soul, and Spirit

Scriptures reveal the soul refers to the part of the human being that will live on in eternity, as in Matthew 10:28 ESV.

We live in a <u>body</u>. We have a <u>soul</u>. We live <u>eternally</u> as <u>a spirit</u>.

Three parts of humans: body, soul, and spirit

Body

The body is the outermost part or physical part of a human being. The body can be seen and touched. At the end of a person's life, the physical body is the only part that dies. According to 1 Corinthians 15 (ESV), our physical bodies are perishable and will decay. This will not be the case with our resurrected and glorified bodies (Phil. 3:21 ESV).

Soul

Our soul is the center of our personality. It is an indication of who we are. With our soul, we think, reason, consider, remember, and make decisions. The soul is the seat of our emotions. Because of the soul, we can experience all kinds of emotions like joy, happiness, love, hate, sorrow, anger, and compassion. Our soul also enables us to have different desires like food, drink, and pleasures.

Spirit

Genesis 2:7 (ESV) states that a human was created as a "living soul." The soul consists of the mind, which includes the conscience, the will, and the emotions. The soul and the spirit are tied together, but they can be separated. "For the word of God is living and active and sharper than any two-edge sword, and piercing as far as the division of soul and spirit, of both joints and marrow, and able to judge the thoughts and intentions of the heart" (Hebrew 4:12 ESV).

The spirit cannot be seen or touched. After God formed man out of the dust of the ground, He blew His breath into the body, and the man became a living being. The spirit is our innermost part. It possesses God-consciousness that enables us to contact and communicate with God (John 4:24 ESV, Rom. 1:9 ESV).

Generations

Abraham's seed has carried out the missionary activity in all the nations since Abraham's days' His seed shall be mighty upon the earth, the generation of the upright shall be blessed (Ps. 12:2 ESV).

I lavish unfailing love to a thousand generations. I forgive iniquity, rebellion, and sin. But I do not excuse the guilty. I lay the sin of the parents upon their children and grandchildren. The entire family is affected—even children in the third and fourth generations (Exod. 34:7).

"Father do not provoke your children to wrath" (Eph. 6:4).

Genesis leads us through all the generations of old starting with Adam and Eve, the first father and mother of civilization up to now.

Could you imagine generations who cannot communicate or express themselves? Well, this is going on now and has been since ancient times.

The benefit of wisdom:

"My son, do not forget my teaching but keep my commandments in your heart, for they will prolong your life many years and bring you prosperity. Let love and faithfulness never leave you, bind them around your neck, write them on the table of your heart. Then you will win favor and a good name in the sight of God and man. Trust in the Lord with all your heart and lean not to your own understanding; in all your ways acknowledge him, and he will make your paths straight" (Prov. 3:3–6).

You and I

Professor E.

Far . . . deep
where only
my heart's eye can see
rests spiritual intuition;
that center point
which sees
harmony so inevitable,
discord so impossible.
Existing discoveries
root safe in the eternal cord,
And those unborn
are sure to blossom.

To my children and grandchildren, my precious peas.

Lineage (Family)

And think not to say within yourselves, we have Abraham to our father: for I say to you, that God is able of these stones to raise up children unto Abraham (Matt. 3:9 KJV).

Moments are like small photographic memories in your life, just passing on the panoramic views of the journey with all the layers of vitality.

My DNA and the Trail of Tears

And think not to say within yourselves, We have Abraham to our father: for I say unto you, that God is able of these stones to raise up children unto Abraham (Matt. 3:9 KJV).

Abraham's seed have carried out the missionary activity in all the nations since Abraham's day.

I can trace my lineage to the Trail of Tears walked by my great-grandmother and grandfather.

My DNA and the Trail of Tears/Family Lineage

Most great truths of the word of God do not lie on the surface. You must dig and search for them just as gold might be found at the bottom of a mine or a pearl at the bottom of the sea. Deeper truths of God must be searched out with great diligence and rightfully divided. I yet see the Potter's hand and his marvelous light at the end of each path, knowing that I have a Comforter (the Holy Spirit) that is forever present in me.

With creation came a rapid change and a host of families occupying the earth, from Adam to Abraham, Jacob, and the patriarchs, as well as other tribes, modern tribes, and nationalities across the globe.

I am a part of God's DNA, created in His image. That alone gives me unspeakable joy and assurance that life has only begun in His walk through it all! Knowing that I have a lineage created in God's mind before my conception, I know my life wasn't rehearsed but a sequence in His divine plan and purpose for my life.

Through it all implies my onward traveling across various stations—things, time, people, places—to overcome past barriers, limitations, and other difficult warfare. The road has been narrowing at times to prevent larger blessings from gracing my present.

Through it all! Yet God continues to lead, guide, and direct my paths. From the beginning until the end of a situation, I have learned to press on without stopping because of the love of a faithful and unconditional Savior.

In thy book were written, every one of them, the days that were formed for me, when as there were none of them (Ps. 139 NIV).

The Family: "The Trail of Tears"

Now here I am from the tribes who walked the Trail of Tears yet am still linked to the Volume of Book. God is the ultimate authority. He will one day judge all nations that He had created in his mind before I was and am.

The phrase originated from a description of the removal of the Choctaw Nation in 1831, a name given to the forced relocation and movement of Native American nations from the southeastern parts of the United States, following the Indian Removal Act of 1830. The removal included many members of the Cherokee, Muscogee (Creek), Seminole, Chickasaw, and Choctaw nations (sometime collectively referred to as the Five Civilized Tribes). They were living autonomously in what would be called the American Deep South, among others in the United States, from their homelands to Indian territory in eastern sections of the present-day state of Oklahoma. Many Native Americans suffered from exposure, diseases, starvation, and death en route to their destination. The relocated Cherokee intermarried and accompanied European Americans, free African Americans, and slaves owned by the Cherokee. History continued and renewed the political and military efforts to remove Native Americans from these lands with the passage of the Indian Removal Act of 1830.

Part of my DNA started with my slave ancestors, my maternal and paternal great-great-grandparents Laney and Mobile, who walked the

"Trail of Tears" from the Deep South to Oklahoma. Afterward, they were married.

Pausing and Reflecting

Laney and Mobile had to pursue the battle of overcoming the hardships they endured, and the legacy of survival to create a lineage.

Bittersweet! Then came the birth of my mother.

Family

Controlled environments or behaviors start with parenting. Parents are responsible for child rearing, nurturing, developmental growth, and education. When you are taught to be seen and not heard, it interferes with exercising thoughts and expressions. Expressing and voicing your opinion is prevalent in the world of communication. Knowledge is power. Not being able to communicate or having an invisible or voiceless thought is traumatizing and keeps us poverty-stricken.

The social ill of creative thinking has stagnated generations since ancient days, holding us captive in this millennial generation.

Raising children does not mean just feeding and dressing them or taking them to school or church or play dates. Raising means lifting or elevating them to a higher level of thinking, feeling, and behaving.

Being candid, I have little to say about my father. because our relationship was like a pop-up—it was only when it was convenient for him—but I will piecemeal his story when it is befitting.

My mother, was a beautiful five-feet-ten-inch redbone Indian-looking woman with Brazilian hair that hung like a horsetail. She was a stern and strong woman. She lacked nurturing skills. It was all learned behavior. She had misplaced her ability to smile. Somehow it was detached from her face and replaced with a poker face until her demise.

She lived the Cinderella syndrome, learning the life of abuse!

She married, and she wanted as many children as God would allow. She had eight children that she was so proud of, and out of her eight, she was certain that one would truly love her. She was overwhelmed by the love that all her children displayed toward her. Life was hard, but Mother tried to change a lot of habits she picked up on the farm with limited formal education. In her days, it was plausible. She came from a large family with eleven siblings; but most of them were put up for adoption, and she was one of them. The church friend of the family adopted her, so she was raised as an only child.

To her surprise, she became a part of the household fixture at her new home in Oklahoma on the farm. She lacked love and compassion. The home was ice cold; and the new parents were so strict that at the age of six, she learned to clean, cook, and serve. She was preparing full meals, especially on Sundays, to feed the church folks.

She always had to eat last. When she matured, my mother's workload increased. She spent longer hours on the farm, tending the animals, picking vegetables, working in the meatpacking house and almond orchard, and anything else required. Mother learned to stay invisible until she was called on. That meant she learned to eat breakfast, lunch, and dinner alone after the adults were served and their stomachs were satisfied. Church and horseback riding became her refuge.

Mother told us she married so that she could leave the farm. And at the age of twenty-one, she married the first military man she encountered and proposed to her, which she accepted.

Different from the Cinderella Fairy Tale

The family who adopted her promised her that if anything happened to either one of the adoptive parents, she will inherit a portion of the land and the Almond Orchard, so the paper was drawn to ensure her share. Her adoptive mother died first, and then the farmhouse burned down to the ground, leaving no proof of her entitlement. Her adoptive father remarried and claimed all the properties that she was supposed to inherit.

That truly left a bitter taste in her mind and heart, leaving her desperate and broken.

In 1952, my father and mother and four of my siblings left Oklahoma for Stockton, California. She was also pregnant with a fifth child, born on her birthday, July 12. She loved her like they were twins. Next came me, Oni, and two more siblings.

We always ate first and had three square meals like clockwork. The last four children weren't allowed in her kitchen, so we didn't learn how to cook at home. Cleaning was a horse of different color. It was our only duty, but it came with high expectations, and we learned it well. My mother would walk behind us after our chore was completed to inspect; and if it wasn't up to her liking, she would pick up anything in her path: ironing cord, 2x4 board, broom, or what else she found befitting for punishment.

Our outings were like her on the farm. You were seen but not heard. All she had to do is give us a certain look, and we knew what it meant. I affirm that if this was going on in today's world, they would have called this child abuse. Believe me, she didn't spare the rod, which was truly a by-product of her era. Now I understand with clarity this was part of her lifestyle growing up on the farm. The old cliché "You can only live what you learn" came to my mind.

One of her favorite sayings was "Nothing from nothing leaves nothing."

Growing up in Stockton was hard on Mother. She had been separated from her family and siblings in Oklahoma for decades.

My father took on a new spirit of his own that didn't include family life. He had succumbed to **the fast lane**: gambling, Cadillacs, dress suits, clubbing, womanizing, and booze—what a combination. Keep in mind that he had a gift of gab, and he didn't have a problem getting a woman to take care of him. Dad had what you call a winning personality.

This is the time we stay across the street from the Do-Drop Inn, the neighborhood bar. Of course, he opened it and closed it too. We could see the front door of the bar from our front bedroom window, the many people leaving and coming, the fighting, and all the other ruckuses. Father would stagger out of the bar door, talking trash, with a different woman hanging on his arm or periodically heading home. Mother would keep her eyes peeled at the window. The tears would run down her face, and her eyes would be blood red, almost like she was walking on eggshells. She would anticipate him coming home. The cursing and fighting and the making up were everyday scenes.

When Father started gambling, the first thing he sold was from our house; it was our dinette table. The next thing he sold was our refrigerator and then any household furniture that would sell. The straw that broke the camel's back was when he signed away the pink slip to his car to keep up his lifestyle. That night he staggered home angry. My mother sensed trouble. She called all of us kids and told us to pick up whatever we could find to help protect her from my dad. We had a broom, sticks, mop, and belts to fight off our father. We looked like little soldiers equipped for battle. We whipped him all the way to the alley behind our house and left him lying in a stupor. He never came back to live with us. Time passed, and Mother seemed more at peace. My sister, Mae, no longer had to play the role of my mother's protector. She could be a teenager once again. My mother never allowed herself to engage in another tumultuous relationship.

My mother went from a particular walk to saving grace. She no longer let fear cripple her. She found refuge in the Lord. Now you could find her head down in reverence to El Elyon, the Highest God. Her children would one day piggyback on these prayers for leadership, guidance, protection, and direction in the name of Jesus. She knew the joy of the Lord was her strength. Yet she never mastered the precious gift of forgiveness. Decades came and went. She stayed angry and forgot how to smile or show love and affection toward her children. My mother never reconciled with our father, and he was never allowed to step foot in our home.

During his visitation, he had to blow his horn so we could meet him at his car. He continued to live the lavish lifestyle that he became accustomed to. I loved his Cadillac. That was his car of choice, and it became a staple for him. His car didn't move unless BB King or Bobby "Blue" Bland was playing, and that's how I was introduced to jazz.

Other staples that sojourned with him were things that lay in the truck of his car: sodas, sandwiches, chips, and other stacks, as well as paper towels, toilet paper, fishing gear, guns, and rifles.

He constantly reminded people that he had them in case of an emergency.

He would say, "Oni, I learned survival in the army, and after I was wounded, I became a limousine driver for the dignitary. This is what sparked my love for beautiful long cars, also light-skinned black women with long-flowing hair. Gambling and booze—these mean-spirited things became attached to me. Although I have a winning personality, I lack peace. I am in my seventies now, and my doctor said I must stop drinking, smoking, and all the other habits and addictions I picked up along the way, or my days are numbered quickly. Oni, now my life consists of fishing, in which I find much peace and joy."

A few years later, in December, I was at my mom's house in Stockton, California, addressing and sending out Christmas cards. I enclosed a five-dollar bill on my dad's card. I heard a loud voice. It was my mom. She told me to remove that five-dollar bill from my daddy's card. He didn't deserve it. I sealed it as though I didn't hear her. I returned to Sacramento, California.

I was having dinner in Sacramento one Christmas evening when I received a call from a hospital in Stockton telling me I needed to come and that my father was in critical condition. I came to find out my father was fishing on Christmas Day. He returned home, drew himself a bath, sat in the tub, and had a heart attack.

I arrived at St. Joseph that Christmas night. I entered his room in the ICU. I looked at him and started to pray. Then I talked to him and told him that I loved him too. A few hours passed. At midnight, he sounded off with the death rattle. God had released his spirit. The tasks of calling everyone who knew him, going to his home, and packing up his belongs were a part of my and my siblings' responsibilities.

One day, while I was retrieving his mail, to my surprise, there was the Christmas card I had sent him. He never got the chance to see it, so I got it back.

I didn't know where to take his belongings, so I took most of the items to my mom's. Among them were several pairs of Stacy Adams, his shoe of choice. I lined all his shoes in my mother's room along one side of the wall. When my mother entered her room, she looked at the row of shoes accessorizing her wall, and she paused. She said loudly and angrily, "That SOB made it to my home after all without his feet." All of us present could only decorate the room with laughter.

Now I know, at that time in my life, the Holy Spirit was preparing me for my ministry, which was pre- and post-bereavement service!

Meet Oni Shabazz

This is the story of becoming Oni. I was born and raised in the small town of Stockton, California, where families were Bible battle ready. The community made a difference. We were close-knit. Everyone's families looked after the others who mostly believed in the power of our Lord and Savior Jesus Christ. Church and school were a priority for the children. Most of the families had at least eight children or more. We all had our share of sibling rivalry. There were eight in my family, including me. I dealt more with rivalry from friends and siblings than the other family members. We were all restricted from playing with the other children unless it was at school or church. Mother believed that there were enough of us, her children, to preoccupy our time without the pressure of peers. Most of the time, we played inside our gated fence, apart from a selected few she would let enter from time to time.

When it comes to my life from childhood to preteens, around fourteen, I grew up with certain values instilled in me by my mother. These journeyed in my mind and heart for decades to come. She had so many sayings, such as "Man is like a bus: miss one catch the next and if you have one outfit wash it every night until you could add to it." She didn't believe in borrowing.

However, her ability to apply developmental growth was lacking in our lives. The five stages of development are newborn, infant, toddler, preschool, and school. This includes infancy (two years old), early childhood (nine to eight years of age), middle childhood, and adolescence (twelve to eight years of age). These were key physical stages or milestones, especially the first five years.

My development unfolded like this: I can't recall the first four years. Maybe this was from domestic abuse that draped our household. Honestly, I don't know. But what I do know is it happened, and there was a host of victims like me. I learned to compartmentalize and cope, carrying these scars for decades.

When it comes to my story of school and church, I am going to piecemeal from kindergarten to tenth grade as much as my memory serves.

I loved school. I knew I needed glasses. I couldn't see the words on the blackboard. My teacher gave me a note for my mother informing her that I needed eyeglasses. I threw the note in the garbage before I reached home. The kids at school were so mean and cruel; it aggravated me how they tormented the student wearing glasses. I didn't want any part of this action, and these were the reasons I didn't express my needs to my mom, which affected me, my behavior, and my grades if the assignments came from the blackboard, and books weren't always available on the predominantly black schools. My sister Pauletta was one year older than I. We mostly shared the same class, so it allowed me to keep my grades up. I was smart in many subjects, and I loved studying. That's why I didn't have to do much communicating. The actions of my work validated itself.

My Children

"Train up a child in the way he should go; even when he is old, he will never depart from it" (Prov. 22:6 KJV).

The first tree that appeared from the base of the root to provide seeds that would produce itself is our Lord and Savior. Abba Father loves me so much that He created my children just for me.

We are part of humanity molded and fashioned by God Himself.

Lord, continue to regulate our minds and hearts and make us whole and worthy of your love.

I realize that my children are experiencing their individuality that does not need approval from me or anyone else except God. Not to mention the new wave of millennial children who will never experience the simple things that we did and enjoyed.

It's time to embrace—not hate but love them unconditionally the way God loves us.

The red-table discussion spearheaded by Jada Pinkett was a blessing, something that I could identify with, reflect on, and live by. Our children flourish in their prime; eventually, they will have their own set of values, ideas, and dreams just like generations before them.

Ultimately, the prophets of old had them too, and they came to fruition, as the Bible tells us.

Some of my favorites are Jacob, Isaiah, Jeremiah, and Ezekiel—the dream makers and shakers.

My modern daydream makers are the late Madam Walker, James Baldwin, Martin Luther King, and many other legendary leaders from every walk of life regardless of race, creed, or color. See the acknowledgment section of the book for other exceptional, extraordinary leaders like Angelou, who was raised by her grandmother, and Tyler Perry, who was raised by a strong churchgoing mother and an abusive father who had a similar discipline style to what I endured.

My Faith Begins Here

For most of my life, I felt like I was in free fall, not knowing how deep the hole was or where it would lead me or how it would end. Has anyone out there in the cosmos ever felt like this? Life had its way. I went deep into the threads of my mind that embarked on long-suffering and pain, which created the seed and harvest for the birth of this book, *A Tunnel of Hidden Thoughts Released*.

Learning to provide instructions or means of expression for my thoughts had to be implemented. My life had many turns and twists because of making uninformed choices, not asking the right questions, or simply not questioning anything or verifying information. I know for a fact that silent minds run deep, carrying with them flashbacks and deep roots that only God can heal.

I thank God for the knowledge, wisdom, and understanding; with these resources, we can ultimately provide people and communities the tools to make informed decisions about communicating and releasing thoughts and ideas to bring dreams once deferred to dreams now hoped for or fulfilled. We can fulfill a lifestyle of choices not guided by government handout to keep the poor idle. Hope enables the voice to ring at its highest capability without fear.

We always have surprises lurking around every corner, and yes, we fall, but we get back up. Remember, the race is not to the swift but to the one who perseveres to the end. I don't want to sound cheesy, but I don't want to live my entire life just settling when God's universe has no beginning or end, and the feasts are great.

Once I identified the root, I let go and gave it to God. I understood that this battle wasn't mine, and I knew that he would make Satan my footstool. I no longer need validation from a man. It was a behavioral problem that the Lord would and could handle with all control and power, and He would lead us straight into the very heart of God.

Like a tree planted by the rivers of other veins of waters inhabited by branches and leaves that are constantly living and dying, so new seeds are constantly germinating. The webs of decades that have recycled things in my life can now be shared.

This volume or open confession is nurtured by God and His divine Will for my life. My spirit, body, and soul are driven through God's WORD and bound by his laws of obedience, sacrifice, and trust based on the foundation of grace, mercy, and love.

God's kingdom rings atonement for our inequity paid and bought by the Blood of Jesus. Now I'm justified by his life, burial, and resurrection in parallel with my confession and exception of this truth. I can certainly look forward to His promise of eternity (SALVATION)!

Thoughts come every second, so we are constantly moving forward in life's cycle. In the beginning, God created the heavens and the earth. My faith began here before I was in my mother's womb. Through faith, my sins are forgiven; and my life is yet changing with divine knowledge, wisdom, and understanding. I can flash back and move forward, for faith comes by acquaintance with Jesus and, through Him, God (the Father), Jesus (His only begotten Son), the Holy Spirit (the Comforter) hence the Trinity

furthermore, through Scriptures from the Bible which is the WORD of God.

"So, then faith comes by hearing, and hearing by the WORD of God" (Rom. 10:17 ESV).

Faith is a wonderful model, for it leads us in the spirit to the foot of the cross. Taking into account the sacrifice Jesus made for us, we confess our sins: we receive forgiveness, and our sins are no longer held against us. How significant is faith; without faith, it is impossible to please God.

We walk by faith, we have assurance by faith, we are sanctified through faith, and we live by faith, which allows us to flash back and glance at various paths, especially those that we have sojourned.

My roads are multifaceted, resembling the beauty of gemstones: diamonds, rubies, emeralds, opals, etc. In my life, there are many more of these stones to come, like that of a diamond in the rough taking on the appearance of a prism for the splendor of God's glory.

The treasure chest is open. Life is like flint. It's extremely hard like a diamond; both share a similar structure.

"In the multitude of my thoughts within me thy comforts delight my soul" (Ps. 94:19 NIV).

The Whole Armor of God

"Put on the full armor of God so that you can take your stand against the devil's Schemes. For our struggles is not against flesh and blood, but against the rulers, against the authorities, against the powers of this dark world and against the spiritual forces heavenly realms" (Eph. 6:11–12 KJV).

Ephesians presents the gospel of Jesus Christ as the answer to the brokenness of the voiceless, broken, and poor in spirit in the world. It allows us the only way to see true transformation in the world.

This is a gift of God's grace, a "grant" in the form of "his Spirit," who strengthens us by guiding us to the fullness of grace in Christ, placing the love of God as new humanity unified in love.

May anything that's bothering you be healed, lifted, solved, and relinquished. Let us all keep the whole armor of God on in every position or post—the front line, the foxhole, and the rear—with all God's gear.

"Therefore, put on the full armor of God so that when the day of evil comes, you may be able to stand your ground and, after you have done everything, stand. "Stand firm then with the belt of truth buckled around your waist, with the breastplate of righteousness in place, and with your feet fitted with readiness that comes from the gospel of peace. In addition to all of this, take up the shield of faith, with which you can extinguish all the flaming arrows of the evil one. Take the helmet of salvation and the sword of the Spirit, which is the word of God. And pray in the Spirit on all occasion with all kinds of Prayers and requests. Be alert and always keep on praying for all the Saints" (Eph. 6:13–18 KJV).

Apostle Paul says, "Pray for me, that whenever I open my mouth, words may be given me so that I will fearlessly make known the mystery of the gospel, for which I am an ambassador in chains. Pray that I may declare it fearlessly, as I could" (Eph. 6:19–20 KJV). This is my prayer too. Amen!

A Spiritual Foundation

My spiritual foundation took root from the inside out, it is something I had to search for and develop an unquenchable thirst for, over the decades of my life love, faith, trust and hope atop fasting, thanksgiving, and forgiveness of prayer ushered in by the Holy Spirit climaxed into a personal relationship. It was no longer about me anymore. I had to learn that I couldn't just add Jesus to my list in life but also submit to Him.

Then, my life started changing, and peace stepped in. The old me started dying daily. This new spirit of me took refuge in God. Regardless of the tribulation that came my way, I found real joy over happiness.

I learned happiness comes with its own bag of tricks, and it is short-lived. When trouble comes, it changes the emotional behavior and outlook of happiness versus unspeakable joy.

I learned how to worship the Lord and the true meaning of worship, which is to acknowledge the Lord in all things, esteem with worth or honor, place highest value on, show perpetual gratitude, prostrate, bow down, throw kisses, surrender, and ascribe all credit to our Lord and Savior Jesus Christ.

True fellowship is when we worship the spirit of God that dwells in each of us so that Christ moves us safely, showing us a new way

of life with clear instructions. These instructions help us avoid experiencing pitfalls and taking God's love for granted.

We learn about God's righteousness—His holiness, power, and sovereignty—with whom we are allowed to have a personal relationship with. We praise to show honor and respect to the God we worship through his son Jesus Christ and the Comforter, acknowledging all belongs to Him. To express gratitude and thanksgiving symbolize the peace with God is the only way to operate spiritually and fellowship and meditate on His purpose for us!

God has been so good to us; we have much to be thankful for and so much more to be prayerful of. We have entered years of unrest, unforeseeable outcomes, high political unrest, fight over land, anxiety, and economic shortfalls; and yet God has chosen this time for me to share this old-age problem of communication barriers and encourage others.

My story is told through renewal, restoration, faith, hope, love, and survival of all aspects of the human condition and calling on the only name under the sun that will and can bring about a perfect change in my life: Jesus!

Ladies and gentlemen, we have an epic deliberation ahead of us, one that at times appears harder than usual, but I want to tell you our reward will be great: salvation!

The Great I Am comprehends us in all frailty and complexity. No details of living lives are hidden from God.

In every day, hour, minute, and second, God allows the light and His grace and mercy to restore and shine in the deepest reservoir of our soul. The gift that cost Jesus his life on earth was for our sins.

God is the Blessed and only Ruler, the King of kings, Lord of lords, who alone is immortal and who lives in unapproachable light, whom no one has seen or can see. To Him be honor and glory forever. Amen!

Transition of Faith

Learning how to worship became key for me. My experience was inevitable.

This is my transition from Christianity to Islam and back to Christianity. I was raised in a Baptist Church around the age of twelve, and I was also Baptist. Little did my mother know when she sent us to church and gave us children money for an offering, it never hit the offering plate. Our Sundays were times we went to the theater. These were a bit of freedom from the gated fence. Yes, we played hooky!

At seventeen, I moved into my first apartment, so I had to learn quickly how to budget and pay bills. Here I was, seventeen years old with a baby, trying to nurture my child properly—what a travesty. I imitated what I learned from my experience at home under my mother's care, but it wasn't enough.

I was introduced to the Nation of Islam. At that time, it was a blessing. I was excited about the classes they held for Muslim girls in training. On top of this, I started learning to love myself and all the other things important in parenting and keeping house. I learned to cook, can, and sew and achieved higher education. These things were important to me. How to eat to live.

The idea of being an entrepreneur enlarged my vision to one day starting and growing a business. The Nation of Islam had many pros. I learned my value and worth. The flipside was I became confused about my feeling toward others. See, I learned from my mother that we are all children of God the Creator.

Eventually, I was like the prodigal son who knew my way back home. Thank god, I piggybacked off my mother's prayers. My life was renewed. The only difference was that I came up with a new agenda. I kept the positive things I learned from Islam under my belt because a holistic lifestyle was a prerequisite for me.

After decades, I met Jesus again, knowing that the word of God is woven in me, the fabric of life. I continue to advocate for God's purpose and plan for my life. Practicing His walk here on earth takes me from glory to glory.

Victory is ours through God's grace, mercy, and goodness!

The Book

I pick up the Bible Book
The devil shook
The believer looked
The unbeliever got cooked
Jesus took the book back with stretched arms
He hollers to his good and faithful servants
Job well done!
But Doon and bloom for the rest of you!

Prayer

The Lord's Prayer appears in two of the four gospels: Matthew (6:9–13 NIV) and Luke (11:2–4 NIV).

"Simply prayer changes things!"

It has been simplified for me to this extent: A prayer is a dialogue between two persons who love each other. It's also an earnest request, entreaty, supplication, or an utterance, as to God, in praise, thanksgiving, etc.

This is a basic prayer—**the Lord's Prayer.**

"And it came to pass, that, as he was praying in a certain place, when he ceased, one of his disciples and he said unto him, Lord teach us to pray, as he touch his disciples" (Luke 11:1 KJV). "And he said unto them, 'Our Father, who art in heaven, hollowed be thy name; thy kingdom come; thy will be done on earth as it is in heaven. Give us this day our daily bread; and forgive us our trespasses as we forgive those who against us, and lead us not into temptation, but deliver us from evil. For thine is the kingdom, and the glory forever and ever. Amen'" (Luke 11:2–4 KJV).

Beatitudes

"Looking at his disciples, he said, 'Blessed are you who are poor, for yours is the kingdom of God'" (Luke 6:20 KJV).

"Blessed are you who hunger now, for you will be satisfied. Blessed are you who weep now, for you will laugh" (Luke 6:21 KJV).

"Blessed are you when people hate you when they exclude you and insult you and reject Your name as evil, because of the Son of Man" (Luke 6:22 KJV).

"Rejoice in that day and leap for joy, because great is your reward in heaven. For that is how their ancestors treated the prophets" (Luke 6:23 KJV).

From a Christian perspective, the Beatitudes teach that people are blessed even in hard times because they will receive eternity in heaven. There are eight of them, and they were the introduction to the Sermon on the Mount (or Beatitude Mountain).

When Jesus saw the crowd, he went to a mountainside and sat down. The disciples came to him, and He began to teach them.

The Beatitudes

He said:

Blessed are the poor in spirit, for theirs is the kingdom of heaven.

Blessed are those who mourn, for they will be comforted.

Blessed are the meek, for they will inherit the earth.

Blessed are those who hunger and thirst for righteousness, for they will be filled.

Blessed are the merciful, for they will be shown mercy.

Blessed are the pure in heart, for they will see God.

Blessed are the peacemakers, for they will be called children of God.

Blessed are those who are persecuted because of righteousness, for theirs is the kingdom of heaven.

Blessed are you when people insult you, persecute you and falsely say all kinds of evil against you because of me. Rejoice and be glad, because great is your reward in heaven, for in the same way they persecuted the prophets who were before you. (Matt 5:1–12)

The purpose of the Beatitudes is to inspire Christians to live according to the traits Jesus describes. They form the cornerstone for an ideal lifestyle in Jesus's walk and serve as the foundation of Christian faith.

These are also a set of teachings and blessings.

Fruits of the Spirit

Let them shout for joy and be glad, who favor my righteous cause, and let them say continually, "Let the Lord be magnified, who has pleasure in the prosperity of His." Hiding emotions can become an art form and superficial, so let's explore some good fruits.

"FRUITS: THERE ARE NINE FRUITS OF THE SPIRIT. Love, joy, peace, patience, kindness, goodness, faithfulness, gentleness, self-control" (Gal. 5:22–23 NIV).

"Taste and see the Lord is good; blessed is the one who takes refuge in Him." - Psalms 34:8 NIV

It is a blessing for me to know I can count on the Lord, who empowers us with these fruits to apply to our everyday lives. They alone keep us challenged in our minds and hearts!

"And my tongue shall speak of your righteousness and of your praises all day long" (Ps. 35:28 NIV).

The fruits are like the diamonds of the first water, blanketing us in comfort and promises, promoting a whirlwind of thoughts and ideas of goodwill.

Thank your human kindness. Let your word be the fruit of your lips.

Let's tap into the six senses. God gives us eyes to see, ears to hear, nose to smell, hands to touch, tongue to taste, and proprioception.

These are also learned behaviors!

Taste, smell, vision, hearing, touch, and awareness of one's body in space? Yes, God has graced us with these gifts. A new study suggests that the last one, called proprioception, may have a genetic value that refers to how the brain understands where the body is in space.

The Road to Salvation

"Therefore, since we have been justified by faith, we have peace with our God through our Lord Jesus Christ" (Rom. 5:1 NIV).

The good news of salvation, the forgiveness of sins, is available to anyone who will trust in Jesus Christ.

We have free will to choose our destiny. God will not force salvation on anyone. Your choice is set before you to accept: heaven or hell and the wide or narrow road. With the acceptance of Jesus, we become part of the Trinity family: God, the (Son) Jesus Christ, and the Holy Spirit the Comforter.

Overall, you become a Christian; and you are born again and sanctified (washed clean as snow), taking on a nature of God your Heavenly Father, which is life. But the nature of sin and Satan is death.

Jesus spoke to the people of His day and spoke in John 8:44, "Ye are of your father the devil. Satan is called . . . the god of this world."

John 3:16 says, "For God so loved the world, that he gave his only begotten Son, that whosoever believeth in him should not perish but have ever-lasting life." Sin was the reason Jesus walked on earth as a man, died on the cross, and experienced hell for one reason to pay the ransom for sin.

Once that price was paid, Jesus Christ was raised from the dead, triumphant over Satan, and the sin issue was taken care of. Heaven has it recorded that you have been set free by the blood of the Lamb.

Although God sent Jesus to pay for your sin and He holds nothing against you, you still can go to hell because you have not decided to make Jesus as your personal Lord and Savior and accept His sacrifice as yours. We learn from Apostle Paul the steps needed for salvation and the results.

The Path to Salvation

"For we have all sinned and fall short of the Glory of God" (Rom. 3:23 NIV).

"For the wages of sin is death but the gift of God is eternal life in Jesus Christ our Lord" (Rom. 6:23 NIV).

"But God demonstrates His own love for us in this: while we were sinner, still sinners, Christ die for us" (Rom. 5:8 NIV).

"If you declare with your mouth, 'Jesus is Lord,' and believe in your heart that He raised Him from the dead you will be saved" (Rom. 10:9 NIV).

"For everyone who call on the name of the Lord will be saved" (Rom. 10:13 NIV).

God's word is the only proof you have that you are saved, but this is the only proof you need.

Songs

Speak to one another with psalms, hymns, and spiritual songs.

Sing and make music in your heart to the Lord, always giving thanks

To God the Father for everything.

In the name of our Lord Jesus Christ. (Eph. 5:19–20 NIV)

"Praises it what I do. Worship is what God expects from me and you."

Worshiping through songs, I found myself gravitating to certain songs and enjoying them immensely over others. I realize I could feel God's presence in those songs.

"Sending Up Timber" is an excellent resource that not only affirms the potency of prayer but also encourages communion with God daily and inspires us to seek and deepen our prayer life. Prayer comes in all forms; meditation, recitation of God's word, praise, songs, and hymns.

Speak to one another with psalms, hymns, and songs from the Spirit. Sing and make music from your heart to the Lord, always giving thanks to God the Father for everything in the name of our Lord Jesus Christ. And the Bible records many songs, especially in the book of Psalms. Listening to the late Curtis Mayfield's music, I found spiritual undertones and a seer's platform. So inspiring, I'm learning how to listen!

Praise the Lord!

"Walk with Me." Listening to this beautiful song!

It left me hypothesized in the spirit. I felt the spirit jump on me!

Song by Songwriter or Author: Joss Stone

As I slay in the spirit, the engine starts. All I could do is reflect on the fantastic journey my Lord and Savior Jesus Christ walked, and I am not stoppin'!

The song reminds me of all the benefits we have as children of God Almighty.

Through every wrong path, pain, reoccurring nightmare, death, and grief, there is a bridge that restores us and refreshes us in the name of Jesus. Step by step, He leads us by the trees of the still waters; and the roots reunite our thought. He lets us know this too shall pass and prepares us for the next to follow and press on for His purpose for life. Worship is based on knowledge or experiences you have about something, person, place, or thing.

I too have a new song once I came through my house fire with limited loss. Because I called on the name of Jesus for help, my hair caught on fire; but my scalp in some places also one side of my forehead with minor burns and nor my forehead had minor burns which healed in a few months and my hair grew back longer than before. The gratitude I felt for Jesus, the name above all names. He gave me a revelation I didn't have to make it. The fire was devastating and out of control. I could have been consumed and my home too, but the Lord heard my cry.

"He covered me!"
Lord, you covered me through the fire
through the fire, Oh Lord, you covered me
thank you, faithful Lord, full of Mercy
You covered me like the three Hebrews boys
My God is inflammable thank you Lord for your grace
You covered me!

Worship is the key reserved for the Lord, meaning He is the controller.

This is how I got over this block in the middle of my path.

Near

The Lord is near to me
He keeps my heart and mind
shielded with the spear of truth.

Yeah, He's near to me!

My eyes see the rear of sin,
I have no more tears.

Yeah, He's near to me!

So let me celebrate this year end.
I hear the Savior say, do not fear
I am here and you are dear to me.

Yeah, the Lord is near and dear to me!

Goodbye, Punch Bowl

Death and Awareness

"He will wipe away every tear from their eyes, and death will be no more. Neither shall there be mourning, nor crying, nor pain anymore, or the former things have passed away" (Rev. 21:4 NIV).

"Death is swallowed up in victory."

I find freedom in releasing quiet thoughts and flashbacks, and you will too. Flashbacks are no longer a precursor to death or foreshadowing danger.

Although Jesus had taken the sting out of death, this is, was, and will continue to be a powerful message for all ages. Christ died for us, no matter where we are coming or going, no matter our walk of life or nationality. Our heart does not have to be overwhelmed.

His spirit abides in you and me. God is a permanent resident in my tabernacle that He fashioned and molded. We must learn Jesus's walk on earth. It is a source of refuge and protection.

Learning how to think, understand, and formulate thoughts is a priority. Again, life and death are of the tongue.

Changes are inevitable. Everything has a season, whether money, illness, bad times, or good times. These are seasonal slides, and they can't last.

The knowledge and understanding that these things happen and exist promote a heightened awareness in our lives.

"But we do not want you to be uninformed, brothers, about those who are asleep, that you may not grieve as others do who have no hope. For since we believe that Jesus died and rose again, even so through Jesus, God will bring with him those who fallen asleep. For this we declare to you by a word from the Lord, we who are alive, who left until the coming of the Lord, will not precede those who fallen asleep. For the Lord himself will descend from heaven with a cry of command, with the voice of an archangel, and with the sound of the trumpet of God. And the dead in Christ will rise first. Then we who are alive, who are left, will be caught up together with them in the clouds to meet the Lord in the air, so we will always be with the Lord" (1 Thess. 4:13–18 NIV).

"And many of those who sleep in the dust of the earth shall awake, some to everlasting life, and some to shame and everlasting contempt" (Dan. 12:2 NIV).

Grief

We know death is inevitable. Moving beyond grief is a must. Other names for *grief* are *mourning*, *grieving*, and *bereavement*. Grief shouldn't always be private but shared.

There is a host of people who have been through what you're going through. They will tell you that you aren't alone. The thoughts may linger, but in due season, the pain will subside. Abba Father says this too shall pass. Be open to counseling and surround yourself with friends and loved ones. Keep in mind that isolation can be detrimental to your health if it stays hidden for a prolonged period.

I was grief-stricken for five years with an *avalanche effect.*

I carried the pain in my heart and mind. *Grieving* took me on an avalanche of an emotional whirlwind that kept me broken and unstoppably crying in a sea of utter darkness.

I tried to numb or mask my feelings with drugs or prescribed meds to keep my thoughts quiet. I stayed in bed for days at a time in a state of depression. When I was awake, I talked to whoever who would listen that it became so repetitive. I lost many friendships; I had become drunken with negativity. This was a pattern for five years.

I became paranoid. I started isolating myself. My decision-making ability was hit hard, and I became gullible to every prey. Holidays and birthdays were the worst. I found myself reliving different events.

I lived in the picture albums, holding pictures to my heart. I also found myself at the cemetery just crying, not knowing what to say or how I should feel. I was emotionally, mentally, and physically drained. I was in deep sorrow, and it was serious.

We know there is no timetable for grief, yet my actions became alarming. I was experiencing everything from anger to denial, to guilt and regret, to sadness and despair, to shock and confusion, to thoughts of suicide and overeating.

Healing

"For I am the Lord who heals you."

"I will give you back your health and heal your wounds. Therefore confess your sins to each other and pray for each other so that you may be healed. The prayer of a righteous person is powerful and effective."

When you are experiencing something in your body, don't speak about what you feel. Speak with what the word says. When you begin to use God's method of calling what you desire (Rom. 4:7 NIV), your body will begin to respond to your faith and demand healing to come forth.

The gifts of healing are among the spiritual gifts listed in 1 Corinthians 12. As an extraordinary charism, gifts of healing are supernatural entitlements given to believers to minister various kinds of healing and restoration to individuals through the power of the Holy Spirit. In the Greek version of the New Testament, both words, *gift* and *healing*, are plural.

Ephesians presents the gospel of Jesus Christ as the answer to the brokenness of the voiceless/broken in the world. It allows us the only way to see true transformation in the world. This is a gift of God's grace—a "grant" in the form of "his Spirit," who strengthens us by guiding us to the fullness of grace in Christ, placing the love of God as new humanity unified in love.

My <u>healing</u> came in the form of an <u>earthquake</u>, a sudden release of stress and a series of trauma that remained captive in my heart and mind, hidden in my earthen vessel. The continuous motion and build-up released in a sudden jerky movement.

The effects of my earthquake were spiritual ground shaking, ground rupture, landslides, tsunamis, and liquefaction. The waves of pain and sorrow that I kept capsulated in my heart over decades reared their ugly head in physical and mental retaliation. Because of my inability to express my feeling audibly, my confidence was damaged, and I destroyed my self-worth. I got caught up in accusing myself.

What I found out was the Holy Spirit that dwells in me kept me through it all. I had to relearn certain habits that became mainstays. It didn't happen overnight. The old me had to die spiritually to put the new me to work.

Now I can speak. I have a voice; Abba Father gave me the opportunity to say yes to His will. I tell you He gives us free will to say yah or nay to His will. I became a shielded vessel for the Lord. I can stand and bind and bond Satan's attacks on me through the Holy Ghost, who is a present help in times of trouble.

I'm challenged and persistent in calling, naming, and recognizing the spirit that tries to beset me. Whether depression, suppression, anger, denial, blame, shame, and regrets, these cause problems for humans by rupturing things in the body—high blood pressure, diabetes, heart attack, kidney issues, blindness, and amputations—wreaking havoc on the quaking that can lead to death. I am telling you what I experienced in my body and an awesome God who has healed me and made me whole for His glory!

I serve a God who loves us unconditionally. I no longer must keep secrets or hide or feel like my life is about to collapse. I've learned I can't hide from God who is omniscient, omnipotent, and omnipresent.

God is omniscient; God knows *everything*. God, "you have searched me and known me" and "you discern my thoughts from afar."

God's all-knowing nature should be comforting to us.

God is omnipresent; God is *everywhere*. "If I go up to the heavens, you are there; if I make my be in the depths, you are there."

God is omnipotent; God is *all-powerful*. "God's "work is wonderful." He knits me.

Relocating from Las Vegas to California

While in Las Vegas before my relocation to Visalia, I heard in my spirit it's time to move to Goshen. Now, this sounds strange. I knew I was going to move; death was all around me. A person I had adopted like a biological niece, Paulette, had lost her only daughter we called Joy.

When I met Joy, she was three years old. She loved mocking me when I would talk, and she would sound just like me. Joy had just graduated from high school and secured her first job and apartment. I was so proud of her. Paulette, her mom, was critically ill; she started losing weight rapidly. She called and told me that Joy had been murdered at her apartment after returning home that night from work. This took place on December 17, 2017.

I couldn't wrap my head around it, so I threw the phone across the room. I had to pray and get my mind together, and I called her back to make sure I heard it right. I had done three funeral services prior to this.

Simultaneously, I was a caregiver for her uncle John who had saved my life eight years prior. He was also in critical condition at the time.

Paulette was so devastated; denial and anger were on the top of the list. I am a pre- and post-bereavement counselor; but because I hadn't buried any children of my own, it was hard for me to counsel her.

The Holy Spirit reminded me of my dear friend and family from Sacramento to come and minister to her here in Las Vegas. When Minister Linda arrived, we picked Paulette up at the house of her cousin, who lived a few blocks from me. I introduced both to each other. Paulette hollered, "Oni"—that's what she always called me—"quit playing with me." She said, "This can't be a minister, looking like Diana Ross with those six-inch heels." We returned to my house, and I gave them some privacy. Then I heard praying and praise and joined them in a night full of praise and prayers. Minister Linda started singing the song "God Is Preparing You." Several hours passed. I asked Paulette if she was ready to go back to her cousin's house. She said no. Paulette ended up staying with me for the next two weeks. Minister Linda returned to Sacramento three days later.

Next, I received a call from Oklahoma. My brother had cancer. He was doing hospice at his son's house. They said he could go at any time. I called him and told him I loved him, but God loved him more. The next day, I got the call that he crossed over. I shared the news with Paulette because I needed to grieve and thank God for taking him home. But I didn't want it to be uncomfortable for her. Paulette responded, "Oni, we are going to grieve together." On February 17, 2018, Paulette moved back to her house.

My New Town

"All these cities were fortified with high walls, gates, and bars, besides a great many unwalled towns" (Deut. 3:5 NIV).

It was May 2018. I moved to my new home in Visalia. On June 29, 2018, I was just removing the last of my boxes from the storage when I received the news of John's death. He lived in Las Vegas.

Afterward, I experienced multiple deaths in my extended family. It took me two years to settle in my new town.

Birds chirped in the brisk morning air; there was nothing like a strong cup of coffee while I unpacked. I enjoyed Mother Nature and wondered what my new town has to offer.

I explored Visalia. It is the crown jewel of the San Joaquin Valley, and it's in the county of Tulare. In Tulare County, dairy remains king.

In Visalia, like anywhere else, people are still getting married, and people are dying. Weddings and funerals are like life and death in a nutshell, but COVID-19 has been the forerunner.

Nothing is quite what I expected but God, and He is my only constant. Visalia may be exactly what I need for a retreat from the fast lane of Las Vegas.

Everything moved slowly. I found peaceful neighborhoods surrounded by stores, eating venues, malls, medical buildings, hospitals, etc. It took less than ten minutes to reach any of these destinations. That was a cakewalk for me!

Acknowledgments

"Nobody cares how much you know until they know how much you care" (Theodore Roosevelt).

"Believe you can, and you're halfway there" (Theodore Roosevelt).

I am acknowledging every leader on every rung of a ladder or level, living or deceased.

From the top to the bottom, in our Lord's sight, there is no ***big I*** and ***little you***. I will mention a few of my heroes and sheroes who strengthened me in one way or another. I am humbled by their wisdom, knowledge, understanding, and mentorship, as well as their ideas, courage, integrity, outstanding achievements, and noble qualities. This is in no particular order with one exception, and that's Jesus.

From the Bible, we also have Jacob's ladder in ancient times, which looks like our DNA. This was the "bridge" between heaven and earth. The ladder in Jacob's story brought him nearer to God.

Leaders always require courage to make ready nations. But God's leadership in us throughout the kingdom. Our first leader is the master leader who has all the power in His hands, our Lord and Savior Jesus Christ.

Lastly, thanking Sharon B., Eleanor and Marquist for their time

Thank you all for your labor and service to others!

I am giving honor to my Heavenly Father, who is all and all, the beginning and the end, the word of the Bile.

I am giving alms of thanksgiving and gratitude. Amen!

About the Author

Oni Shabazzis the founder/CEO of a pre- and post-bereavement consultant/contract service. She has a master's degree in Christian counseling. She has been involved with funeral arranging and event planning for over thirty-seven years and counting.

She has helped countless families create meaningful ceremonies that also focus on the celebration of a loved one's life.

This company was there to provide timely, efficient, and compassion-oriented service in those difficult times.

My life and journey flash before me now that I have my being.

I know that God is the author and finisher of my life.

We're only here for a moment in time. Our impact is what counts.

The impact you have on the lives you touched is what I feel. His light shining through you is what I see. Dear friend, that seed is yet traveling with me!

Death and dying visited me again from 2015 to 2019. I was once again overwhelmed by the death of my late husband, two sisters, two great-nephews, a niece, a brother, and several friends. Thank You, Lord, for the strength that surpasses all understanding and unspeakable joy.

Don't get me wrong. I felt pain, but I was able to express it and not suppress it. In 2019, I moved to California. In 2020, I was in a house fire, which burned my forehead and hair. I was in an extended stay for almost five months, and I met the place that the Holy Spirit put on my heart and mind. Here came forth the vision for this book, *A Tunnel of Hidden Thoughts Released*. I know I have a purpose in my path. Hallelujah!

Besides her business and visions, Oni is a collector of fine arts and paraphernalia.

She also gains further inspiration from networking and visiting the coast where she has a special affinity for the humbling life force of the ocean. She also finds solace surrounded by the mountains and the city of lights. She enjoys a great movie and good music as well.

Oni concludes by saying there is nothing more endearing than family and the unconditional love of Abba Father and his goodness and mercy. Amen!

Goodbye, Punch Bowl

Shadowboxing is making the motions of boxing—bobbing, weaving, and punching—alone.

The phrase comes from the idea that you are boxing with your shadow, although that would be impossible in the dark.

This is spiritual warfare at its best. I thank God that He is my partner, my all in all, and I am never alone.

At different times in my life, I felt like I was always fighting. I had to empty and divorce myself from toxic behaviors.

A punch bowl is a large bowl for serving punch and other ingredients, usually with a ladle, and often having small drinking glasses hooked around the rim. And in this case, when the punch bowl is empty, spiritual fighting ensues from this negative and evil toxic bowl.

In this narrative, the red punch symbolizes the blood of destruction. The punch bowl gets its name from the cemetery over ten decades ago by a volcano blast that left a crater, giving the punch bowl its unique shape and name.

Today, we are pouring out of these cups of spiritual poison and saying **goodbye**. We have divine power to demolish every stronghold that has consumed our minds and hearts. This journey is about learning to use the word of God (Judges 6:17–23 NIV).

We are free to minister truth and hope and courage to people. Being out of balance creates a state of limbo; the tipping point resonates loudly with the lack of value, humanity, and respect for self and others. We must learn to accept things we cannot change and focus on all the things that God can change. Faith gives us goodness, greatness, mercy, grace, and fortitude to make a spiritual journey with hope and assurance in the Lord.

We must stay fluid in the word with boldness and keep striving for righteousness' sake.

I WITH THERE:

The place call there; all things are stored on a self in my mind, where there, you can't recall and share in laughter, joy, or peace. Just trying to escape from depression and life's reality.

Today is a new time. I'm picking peace over drama and distance over disrespect because God is my reason for the season. I will be like the abstract artist Pietro Adamo, who used strong lines and colors and textures to express his feelings on canvas.

I am conveying my inner self through thoughts, expressions, emotions, feeling, and memories without regret. **Goodbye, Punch Bowl!**

I am divorcing my past, I am divorcing pain, I am divorcing anger, I am divorcing doubt, I am divorcing setbacks, and I am divorcing negative gas-lighting people who want to keep me in the past.

I am divorcing lack; God has given me the power to ***trust in Him*** and release all hidden hurts.

Now my tunnel is full of God's treasure, and *love* is foremost. God has let me reposition myself to things anew, not the *flesh* but the *spirit*.